mason jar
salads *and more*

mason jar
salads *and more*

Julia Mirabella

50 Layered Lunches to Grab & Go

Ulysses Press

Published by
Ulysses Press
P.O. Box 3440
Berkeley, CA 94703
www.ulyssespress.com

ISBN: 978-1-61243-289-2
Library of Congress Catalog Number 2013957328

Printed in Canada by Marquis Book Printing

10 9 8 7 6

Acquisitions editor: Kelly Reed
Managing editor: Claire Chun
Editor: Phyllis Elving
Proofreader: Elyce Berrigan-Dunlop
Front cover design: DiAnna VanEycke
Interior layout and design: what!design @ whatweb.com
Cover photographs: © Julia Mirabella
Index: Sayre Van Young

Distributed by Publishers Group West

To my parents, my favorite sous chefs.

table of contents

introduction

When I started my first job after I'd finished school, I suddenly found that I had a lot less time. I was busy at work, working late hours, and eating out every day for lunch. A few months into the job, I realized that something had to change. There was nowhere to get a salad or anything healthy near my office, and every day I found myself eating unhealthy lunches. Meanwhile, the produce I was buying each weekend at the farmers' market was slowly rotting in my fridge. I needed a way to eat healthier — and to make sure I actually ate the healthy foods I was buying.

Eating healthy means eating more fresh produce and home-cooked meals — but making a healthy lunch every day takes time I just don't have. Plus, salads can be tricky to bring to work: you need the right container, and your salad can end up soggy if you add the dressing in the morning, or the night before.

My solution has been to make my salads in Mason jars. By spending a little time on the weekend making Mason jar salads for the coming week, I've solved many of the difficulties of bringing my lunch to work — and fresh produce no longer languishes in my refrigerator. Most salads will stay fresh for 4 or 5 days in the fridge in their Mason jars, and I can just grab a jar as I head out for work each morning.

Of course, I couldn't stop with salads! I've expanded my Mason jar menus to include everything from pastas to soups, smoothies, and salsas. You'll find all sorts of lunchtime options in these pages, plus breakfasts and snacks. There's no magic formula for making Mason jar meals — the recipes in this book are here to give you a few ideas and get you started. Mason jar meals are about finding ways to save time and eat healthy. Don't stress about following the recipes perfectly. Experiment with your own favorite ingredients — and have fun!

TIP

Mason jar salads are perfect to take to work, but they're useful for much more, too. They are a great way to give new parents a few fast and fresh meals, for example, or to leave dinner for your babysitter or bring salad to a friend's barbecue.

How Do Mason Jar Salads Work?

A Mason jar salad works by using the jar's verticality to your advantage. The trick is to layer your salads instead of mixing all of their ingredients together.

You start by layering the salad dressing on the bottom of the jar. Next come your salad's firmer vegetables — bell peppers or carrots, for instance. When you add salad greens on top, this layer of firm vegetables keeps the moisture of the dressing away from the greens, so they won't wilt.

Mason jars also let you pack your salads tightly. That means there isn't much air left in the jars, so salad ingredients stay fresh longer.

Mason Jar Benefits

portion control: Mason jars make it easy to control the size of your lunches. Portion control helps stop you from overeating and lets you stay true to a program of healthy eating.

saving time: You can make several Mason jar salads all at once on a Sunday — an hour's effort that will see you through the coming work week.

saving money: Mason jars aren't expensive. A set of 12 costs about $15, and the jars can be used over and over again. Furthermore, being able to make the salads ahead of time means that you're more likely to eat the produce you buy. This saves you money, because you won't be letting food go bad.

easy cleanup: Mason jars are a snap to wash. At the end of the day, just deposit the jars and lids in the dishwasher and they'll emerge squeaky clean.

glass is best! Glass jars don't absorb germs from food, since their surface isn't porous. This means that glass containers can be fully sterilized in a dishwasher. And with glass, you avoid the concerns over toxins being transferred to food from plastic containers.

airtight seal: Once the top is screwed onto a Mason jar, you have an airtight seal. You don't need to worry about food spilling into your bag on the way to work.

What Do You Need?

You don't need much in the way of equipment to start making these salads. A few tools go a long way.

mason jar: A jar, of course, is the only real requirement for a Mason jar salad. I use pint- or quart-size jars, and I highly recommend the wide-mouth type. They make it easy to get your ingredients into the jars without making a mess.

Mason jars are readily available at grocery and hardware stores. A dozen jars will cost you around $15. They have countless other uses, too, so you'll definitely get your money's worth. I carry coffee and tea to work in Mason jars, use them to hold pens on my desk, and have one on my bathroom counter as a toothbrush holder.

canning funnel: Canning funnels are especially helpful if you're making your salads in regular rather than wide-mouth jars. A funnel makes it so much easier to ensure your food goes into the jar instead of onto the counter, keeping the whole process mess-free. Usually sold right alongside Mason jars, canning funnels can be purchased for around $5. They are dishwasher safe, and many are collapsible.

salad spinner: Minimizing the moisture in your salad greens is key to creating a successful Mason jar salad. Salad spinners are essential for this; I can't do without one.

spatula: One of my favorite kitchen tools is a long, slender spatula called the Scrape and Scoop, made by Tovolo. Because it's narrow and reaches farther than your fingers can, it's perfect for moving ingredients around in a Mason jar.

salad bowl and fork: The final utensils you'll need are a salad bowl and a fork that you can keep at your workplace, or wherever you'll be eating your Mason jar salads. It's not easy to eat these salads straight out of the jar, so it's best to have a bowl on hand.

Assembling Mason Jar Salads

The most efficient way to make Mason jar salads is to assemble more than one at a time, maybe even enough to take to work each day of the following week. Try to make similar types of salads at the same time — it cuts down on costs, since you don't need to buy many different ingredients. But make sure to have enough variety that you won't get tired of eating the salads day after day.

1: Begin by washing your salad ingredients and cutting the vegetables or fruits as needed. Choose a few vegetables that can be used in all of the salads you're making. It's good to have a few firm veggies to layer at the bottom of the jar.

2: The secret to a Mason jar salad is *layering*. Start with the dressing on the bottom. I use about 3 to 4 tablespoons of salad dressing per quart jar, or 2 tablespoons per pint jar. (I've also found it helpful to place onions at the bottom, if I'm using them, because soaking them in the dressing helps dilute the strong onion taste and prevents onion breath at work.)

3: Next add some salad ingredients that won't soak up the dressing, such as carrots, cherry tomatoes, sugar snap peas, or chickpeas.

4: Continue to layer your salad with your chosen ingredients. Pack the layers as tightly as possible — the less air between layers, the longer your salad will stay fresh.

5: Finally, layer on your salad greens. By ending with the greens at the top, you'll create a moisture barrier that prevents the entire salad from becoming soggy. If you are including cheese and/or nuts, add them last.

6: Twist on the tops to seal your salads, place the jars in your refrigerator, and you're good to go! If you want to include a protein such as chicken, just place it on top of the salad greens in the morning on the day you'll eat the salad.

7: When you're ready to eat the salad, just pour it into a bowl and toss to mix the dressing into the salad.

Reheating Food in Jars

Some of the recipes in this book are best eaten after they have been reheated. You can microwave all the lunches in the Mason jars, though it works best for the soups and oatmeal. For pastas and other lunches, I recommend placing them in a bowl or on a plate to allow for more even reheating.

The Parchment Paper Fix

Some of the best salads don't include any firm vegetables, and this can be problematic when it comes to layering your salad dressing at the bottom of the jar. Fruits, for example, will soak up the vinegar in dressing. At least one company sells reusable cups that fit into the tops of Mason jars, providing one solution. But for a quick and inexpensive fix, all you need is parchment paper, or even plastic wrap.

1: To use the parchment paper fix, layer your salad in the jar as usual but leave out the dressing. Instead of filling the jar all the way up, leave some space for dressing at the top.

2: Cut out a square of parchment paper that's about a couple of inches wider than the jar top on all sides (an 8 x 8-inch square is more than enough). Place it over the jar and push down to form a little cup. The edges of the parchment paper should extend beyond the edge of the jar; bend them down toward the outside of the jar.

3: Pour your salad dressing into the parchment paper cup and twist on the lid. The jar will stay sealed, even over the parchment paper. Just make sure the lid is on tight, and nothing should leak. (However, I don't recommend leaving the salad upside down.)

4: When it's time to eat, just dump the dressing into your bowl, empty the contents of the jar into the bowl, and toss your salad.

A Few Pointers

vinaigrettes: I've found that vinaigrettes are the best dressings to use in Mason jar salads. Many other salad dressings will separate, if they sit for too long. You can make vinaigrettes quickly and inexpensively, and if they separate, it's easy to whisk them back together.

All of the salads in this book are accompanied by a vinaigrette. You'll find the recipes for these dressings in the last chapter of the book.

proteins: Many of the Mason jar meals in this book don't include meat, but you can easily add chicken, steak, or some other protein. I recommend adding them to your salad on the day you plan to eat it, rather than letting them sit in the jar for several days.

vacuum seal: The biggest reason that salad greens go bad is air in the container. To prevent this, some people use a vacuum sealer with a jar attachment. Investing in such a sealer to remove the air from the jar will certainly help your salads stay fresh longer, though the sealer is a bit pricey. If you don't want to buy a vacuum sealer, no problem! Just make sure that the jar is full of vegetables and that everything is packed tightly together. The less space at the top of the jar, the less air you'll have in it.

breakfasts

It's easy to skip breakfast on mornings when you get up late and need to dash out the door quickly. These breakfasts are designed to help you with the morning rush. You can make one in minutes before you head to work, or you can make a week's worth of breakfasts on a Sunday night.

banana and almond butter smoothie

I only recently started using almond milk in smoothies, and now I'm addicted. Bananas go particularly well with almond milk, and this smoothie—packed with protein from the almond butter and fiber from flaxseed—is a perfect way to get going in the morning. If you have an immersion blender, you can mix it right in your Mason jar and then get started on your morning commute.

Makes 1 smoothie

1 cup plain almond milk
1 tablespoon almond butter
1 tablespoon ground flaxseed
1 banana, fresh or frozen
1 pint-size Mason jar

Blend the smoothie ingredients together in a food processor or blender, then pour into the Mason jar. Or place the ingredients directly in the jar and use an immersion blender. Seal the jar to drink your smoothie on the go or at work. This smoothie is best made the morning of. If the smoothie separates, just shake it up in the jar before drinking it.

Bananas on Ice

Frozen bananas are a great way to chill a smoothie without using ice, and they're easy to prepare. Simply place a fresh banana in the freezer overnight. The next day the outer skin will be brown, but the frozen fruit inside will still be perfect. Frozen bananas will last about 4 months in the freezer.

To use, remove the banana from the freezer and let it sit for 5 minutes. Then cut off the top and bottom ends, slice the banana in half lengthwise, and peel off the skin. Place the peeled, frozen banana pieces in the blender with your other smoothie ingredients.

blueberry breakfast smoothie

Blueberries are not only super tasty, they're also rich in antioxidants. I try to consume them any way that I can. This simple smoothie also includes a tablespoon of flaxseed, giving you a good dose of fiber and omega-3 fatty acids. Yum!

Makes 1 smoothie

1 cup skim milk or plain soy milk

½ cup blueberries

1 tablespoon ground flaxseed

1 banana

1 pint-size Mason jar

Add the skim or soy milk, blueberries, and flaxseed to the container of a blender or to the Mason jar. Peel the banana and break it into pieces, then add it to the other ingredients. Purée in the blender and transfer to the Mason jar, or purée directly in a pint-size jar using an immersion blender. Seal.

green smoothie

Yes, this smoothie is green, but don't let the color stop you. It tastes amazing, and it's really good for you. First of all, it includes high-fiber kiwi fruit, which also provides a dose of vitamin C and antioxidants. Next you have spinach, giving you iron and zinc. Add apple or pear juice and you have a sweet and nutritious concoction that your body will appreciate.

This smoothie can be made the night before, though it is best to make it in the morning. If the smoothie separates overnight, just shake it up to mix it back together.

Makes 1 smoothie

1 kiwi fruit
½ apple, peeled and cored
1 cup pear or apple juice, plus more as needed
½ cup spinach leaves
1 pint-size Mason jar

Cut the kiwi fruit in half lengthwise and scoop out the flesh with a spoon. Cut the half apple into chunks and place in the blender along with the kiwi fruit, 1 cup pear or apple juice, and the spinach. Blend until smooth, adding more juice if needed to reach the desired consistency. Transfer your smoothie to the Mason jar and seal to take to work.

peach and strawberry smoothie

This smoothie tastes like summer in a glass. Peaches and strawberries go beautifully together, and adding a little orange juice and honey makes the pairing perfect. If you want to make this drink even more nutritious, add the chia seeds for omega-3 fatty acids, calcium, and manganese. Just make sure you don't get the seeds stuck in your teeth!

Makes 1 smoothie

1 cup orange juice

1 peach, peeled and cut into pieces

½ cup strawberries

1 tablespoon chia seeds (optional)

1 teaspoon honey (optional)

1 pint-size Mason jar

In a blender, mix together the orange juice, peach, and strawberries; pour into the Mason jar. Or mix right in the Mason jar using an immersion blender. Stir in the chia seeds and honey to sweeten, if using, and seal the jar.

mango smoothie

This smoothie tastes especially fantastic when mangoes are in season, but you can easily substitute frozen mangoes for the fresh fruit.

Makes 1 smoothie

1 mango, pitted and cut into pieces*

¾ cup carrot juice

1 banana

1 pint-size Mason jar

* For mango-cutting directions, see the recipe for Curry Chicken Salad on page 85.

Use a blender to purée the mango pieces, carrot juice, and banana together. Pour the mixture into the Mason jar, seal, and you're ready to go.

steel-cut oatmeal

Steel-cut oats in a Mason jar is hands down my favorite homemade breakfast for the workweek. If I don't think ahead about my breakfasts for the coming week, I end up making bad choices when I show up at the office hungry and am presented with unhealthy snacks. Bringing oatmeal in a Mason jar has helped change my mornings, giving me a breakfast that starts my day off right.

This recipe uses steel-cut oats, which usually take 20 to 30 minutes to cook. Here the Mason jars help do the cooking for you, so it takes only 10 minutes to make a week's worth of breakfasts.

While oatmeal can seem bland, all it really takes is a little inventiveness with toppings to make it tasty. I'm a big fan of nuts and dried fruits—almonds, raisins, and dried cranberries are favorites—but fresh fruits such as blueberries or strawberries are great, too.

Makes 5 servings

4½ cups water, plus more as needed for reheating
1¼ cups steel-cut oats
toppings of your choice
milk for serving (optional)
honey or brown sugar (optional)
5 pint-size Mason jars

In a saucepan on the stovetop over high heat, bring the 4½ cups water and the oats to a boil. Reduce the heat to medium and simmer for 10 minutes. Remove from the stove and carefully spoon the oatmeal and liquid equally into the 5 jars. (I find a canning funnel to be helpful for this.)

Seal the jars of hot oatmeal and leave them out on the kitchen counter overnight. When you walk into the kitchen the next morning, you'll have 5 jars of cooked steel-cut oats that will last you all week! Place toppings in each jar, or wait to add them each morning.

Take one of the jars to work and refrigerate the others to be used on other days. Once you're at work, add a bit more water (a tablespoon or so) and heat the oatmeal in the jar in a microwave oven. Stir. Add milk and honey or brown sugar, if using, and enjoy!

oats and fruit in almond milk

It's often a little too hot to appreciate warm oatmeal in the summertime. Not to fear, you can enjoy your oats cold, too! You just need to use *rolled* oats instead of steel-cut ones. This recipe requires you to make your meal the night before you'll use it (not a week's worth at once), but there's absolutely no cooking involved. It can't get easier than this for breakfast.

Makes 1 serving

1 cup rolled oats
1½ cups plain almond milk (or milk of your choice)
honey or stevia, to sweeten
berries and nuts for toppings, as desired
1 pint-size Mason jar

Place the rolled oats in the Mason jar and add the almond milk (or whatever milk you're using). Stir the oats and milk together. Seal the jar and refrigerate overnight. In the morning, stir in a sweetener, if using, and add toppings, as you wish.

raspberry and blackberry smoothie

Blackberries can be tart, but they pair well with the sweetness of raspberries and a bit of honey. There can be quite a lot of seeds in this mixture, so you may want to strain your smoothie before you take it to the office.

Makes 1 smoothie

½ cup plain soy milk
¼ cup vanilla yogurt
½ cup blackberries
½ cup raspberries
honey or stevia, to sweeten
1 pint-size Mason jar

Using a blender, purée together the soy milk, yogurt, blackberries, and raspberries. Sweeten to taste with honey or stevia. Strain out the seeds, if desired. Pour into the Mason jar and seal.

salads

I'm a huge fan of farmers' markets. I go to the market near my house every weekend, and it has changed the way I eat, for the better. I'm constantly introduced to new vegetables, and I've begun to eat seasonally — not just by default, but because in-season fruits and vegetables taste wonderful. Mason jar salads have helped me make the most of my market visits.

The salads in this section include many ingredients that start to show up in farmers' markets in the spring and summer. And while many of these salads feature leafy greens such as spinach, arugula, and mesclun, delicious salads can be created with more than just greens. You'll find good grain- and legume-based salads here, too. You can create endless variations of tasty, easy, and convenient Mason jar salads. The following recipes give you a great place to start.

beet and carrot salad

Earthy beets, crunchy carrots, salty pistachios, and soft goat cheese? Bring it on! As summer gives way to fall, it's good to know there are still Mason jar salads to be made and tasty ingredients to go into them (even if they are mostly root vegetables). Yes, when you buy beets they're covered in dirt and have to be cooked, but it doesn't take much to get them ready — and the payoff is well worth the work. If you don't have time to cook the beets yourself, keep an eye out for precooked ones at your local grocery store.

Makes 1 serving

½ cup julienne-cut carrots, about 1 medium carrot (directions below)

3 tablespoons Red Wine Vinaigrette (recipe on page 130)

½ to ¾ cup cubed or quartered cooked beets

2 cups spinach leaves

2 ounces crumbled goat cheese

¼ cup shelled pistachios

1 pint-size Mason jar

Roasting Beets

To roast beets, start by preheating your oven to 425°F. While the oven is heating, trim the tops off the beets, leaving about half an inch of stems at the top. Scrub the beets under cold water to remove any dirt. Place in a baking dish, add about half an inch of water, and put in the oven. Roast 30 to 40 minutes for small beets, 40 to 45 minutes for medium beets, or 50 to 60 minutes for large beets.

The beets are done when you can easily pierce them with a knife. Remove the cooked beets from the oven and let cool. Then — wearing rubber gloves to keep your hands from being dyed beet red — cut off the tops and bottoms and slip off the beet skins.

To cut matchstick-size carrot pieces, cut a carrot in half crosswise and then cut each piece in half lengthwise. Place each section cut-side down on your cutting surface and slice lengthwise into about 4 pieces. Repeat as needed until the pieces are the right size.

Pour the vinaigrette dressing into the bottom of the Mason jar. Add the carrots and then layer on the beets, spinach, and goat cheese. Top with ¼ cup pistachios. Seal the jar and refrigerate until ready to eat.

watermelon and feta salad

Nothing screams summer like watermelon. When it's especially hot out, some cool, sweet watermelon will help you get through the afternoon. This salad adds a savory note with cherry tomatoes and feta, perfectly complementing the flavor of the watermelon without diminishing the cooling effect.

Makes 1 serving

2 to 3 tablespoons Sherry Vinaigrette (recipe on page 131)
1 cup halved cherry tomatoes
⅓ cup roughly chopped fresh parsley
2 cups cubed seedless watermelon
2 ounces crumbled feta cheese
1 pint-size Mason jar

Layer the salad ingredients in the Mason jar, starting with the vinaigrette dressing and continuing with the tomatoes, parsley, watermelon, and feta cheese, in that order. Seal the jar and refrigerate until ready to use.

caprese salad

Caprese salads always remind me of Italy, where you can order caprese throughout the summer and feel as satisfied as if you'd just eaten an intricate and complicated meal. The key to making this salad as flavorful as possible is to choose quality mozzarella and the freshest tomatoes.

Makes 2 servings

2 heirloom tomatoes (I like them to be different colors)
8 ounces fresh mozzarella cheese
4 tablespoons Balsamic Vinaigrette (recipe on page 131)
6 to 8 fresh basil leaves
2 pint-size Mason jars

Slice the tomatoes and the mozzarella cheese horizontally into ¼-inch rounds.

Place 2 tablespoons of vinaigrette in the bottom of each Mason jar. Starting with the tomatoes, layer the salad — tomatoes, mozzarella, and basil leaves — repeating the layers until the jar is full. Seal and refrigerate until ready to use.

corn and blueberry salad

Who knew that corn and blueberries would be so good together? Try this salad and see for yourself! This sweet and tangy combination takes only a little time to put together, and it's easy to eat on the go. Bring it to work for lunch or to a friend's picnic as a side dish. If you want to turn it into a green salad, use a quart-size Mason jar and add 2 cups of mixed greens or spinach on top.

Makes 1 serving

2 ears of corn, for about ¾ cup kernels
1½ tablespoons Lime Vinaigrette (recipe on page 131)
1 to 2 tablespoons finely chopped red onion
½ cup cucumber slices (half- or quarter-moons)
1½ tablespoons chopped fresh cilantro
½ cup blueberries
1 pint-size Mason jar

Remove the husks and silks from the corn. Pour enough water into a pot to cover the corn and bring to a boil over high heat. Add the corn and boil for 5 minutes. Remove the corn from the water and let cool for a few minutes, then slice off the kernels.

Layer the salad ingredients in the Mason jar, starting with the vinaigrette, then the onion and the cucumber. Finish with layers of corn kernels, cilantro, and blueberries. Seal and refrigerate until ready to use.

green bean and feta salad

Brightly colored and with a satisfying crunch, green beans don't need much to improve them—as long as you don't overcook them! Steam or boil your green beans to get maximum flavor out of them.

Makes 1 to 2 servings

3 cups green beans

2½ tablespoons Balsamic Vinaigrette (recipe on page 131)

¾ cup halved cherry tomatoes

¼ cup thinly sliced shallots

6 or 7 basil leaves

2 ounces crumbled feta cheese

1 quart-size Mason jar

Trim the ends from the green beans; cut the beans in half crosswise. Bring a pot of water to a boil over high heat (don't salt the water), add the beans, and boil for 5 minutes. Transfer the beans to an ice-water bath for a minute to stop the cooking process and preserve their color. Drain.

When the green beans have cooled, layer the salad ingredients in the Mason jar, beginning with the vinaigrette and continuing with the tomatoes, shallots, cooked beans, basil leaves, and feta cheese. Seal and refrigerate until ready to use.

barley and zucchini salad

Sometimes I find it nice to have a salad without leafy greens. This barley salad is light and fresh, with crunchy bursts from bell pepper and sweet, bright elements from tomatoes. While a bit of cooking is required—for the barley and zucchini—it's totally worth it to offer your taste buds something a little different.

Makes 1 serving

3 tablespoons olive oil, divided
¼ cup quick-cooking barley, to make ¾ cup cooked barley
½ cup water
salt and black pepper
½ medium to large zucchini
1 tablespoon Red Wine Vinaigrette (recipe on page 130)
½ cup halved cherry tomatoes
½ cup chopped yellow bell pepper
1 pint-size Mason jar

In a small skillet, heat 1 tablespoon of the olive oil at medium heat. Add the barley and, stirring lightly, toast the barley until it is golden brown. Remove from the heat and set aside.

Pour the water into a saucepan, season with a pinch of salt, and bring to a boil over high heat. Add the barley, reduce the heat, and simmer for 20 minutes, covered, until the water has been fully absorbed.

Thinly slice the zucchini half, using a knife or mandolin, and then cut the slices into half-moons. In a skillet, heat the remaining 2 tablespoons of olive oil over high heat and add the zucchini. Cook until the zucchini begins to turn golden brown, then flip the pieces over to finish cooking. Transfer to a paper towel–lined plate to dry out and cool. Sprinkle with salt and pepper.

To assemble the salad, pour the vinaigrette into the Mason jar. Place the tomatoes in the dressing at the bottom of the jar. Add ½ cup of the cooked barley in a single layer, pressing it down a bit with the back of a spoon to make room for the remaining ingredients. Add the zucchini, then fill the rest of the jar with the bell pepper. Seal the jar and refrigerate until ready to use.

sorrel and peach salad

Don't be afraid to experiment with different ingredients and make use of your farmers' markets and the farmers' expertise! This salad was created after a visit to my neighborhood farmers' market, which has a stand that offers about ten different types of salad greens. After chatting with the farmer, I was convinced to try sorrel, which she assured me paired perfectly with peaches. I'm glad I took her advice—the result was this delicious salad.

Makes 1 serving

2 tablespoons Red Wine Vinaigrette (recipe on page 130)

½ teaspoon honey

1 or 2 peaches, peeled and thinly sliced

2 cups sorrel leaves

½ cup roughly chopped pecans

2 ounces crumbled goat cheese (optional)

1 quart-size Mason jar

Whisk the vinaigrette together with the honey in the Mason jar. Layer the rest of the ingredients in the order listed, starting with the peaches and ending with the goat cheese, if using. Then seal the jar, refrigerate, and prepare to enjoy!

> **TIP**
>
> This salad is best when eaten within a day of making it, since the peaches will absorb the dressing as the salad sits. If you want to make it farther ahead, use the parchment paper trick (page 14) to keep the vinaigrette separated from the other ingredients.

pea shoot and radish salad

If you haven't eaten pea shoots, you should definitely try them. These leafy greens have delicate tendrils and a strong pea flavor (I guess that shouldn't be surprising). Pea shoots tend to wilt easily, so try to eat this salad within a couple of days of making it.

Makes 1 serving

2 to 3 tablespoons French Vinaigrette (recipe on page 130)

½ cup julienne-cut carrots*

½ cup radishes, thinly sliced (use a mandolin if you have one)

2 cups pea shoot greens

1 quart-size Mason jar

* See the Beet-Carrot Salad recipe on page 33 for carrot-cutting instructions.

Place the vinaigrette in the Mason jar. Layer the carrots and radishes over the dressing and then fill the rest of the jar with the pea shoots. Seal and refrigerate until ready to use.

southwestern salad

Colorful with lots of protein and antioxidants, this hearty salad will keep you satisfied until dinnertime. You can step it up a notch with a little hot sauce in your salad dressing if you want to make things interesting.

Makes 1 serving

3 tablespoons Lime Vinaigrette (recipe on page 131, with hot sauce, optional)

½ cup black beans, rinsed and drained

½ red vine-ripened tomato, diced

¼ red bell pepper, diced

¼ yellow bell pepper, diced

½ cup diced avocado (optional)

½ cup corn kernels, fresh or frozen

2 cups mixed salad greens

1 ounce Cheddar cheese, grated

1 quart-size Mason jar

Start by pouring the vinaigrette dressing into the Mason jar. Then layer in the black beans, tomato, bell peppers, avocado, and corn. Finish with the salad greens and, finally, the Cheddar cheese. Seal and refrigerate until ready to use.

arugula, pine nut, and parmesan salad

I love arugula! Arugula is one of the most nutritious salad greens you can buy in the supermarket and one of my go-tos. I like making salads that let its peppery flavor shine. Here, arugula is accompanied only by pine nuts, nutty Parmesan cheese, and bright cherry tomatoes.

Makes 1 serving

1 tablespoon olive oil

⅓ cup pine nuts

2 to 3 tablespoons Lemon Vinaigrette (recipe on page 130)

1 cup halved cherry tomatoes

2½ cups arugula leaves

2 tablespoons shaved Parmigiano-Reggiano cheese

1 quart-size Mason jar

Heat the olive oil in a small skillet over medium heat. Add the pine nuts and toast, stirring frequently, until golden brown, for about 3 minutes. Remove from the heat and let cool.

Layer all the ingredients in the Mason jar, starting with the vinaigrette and continuing with the tomatoes, arugula, and pine nuts. Finish the salad with the shaved cheese. Seal and refrigerate, or drop the jar into your bag to take to work.

kale and avocado salad

Kale salads are popular these days, and I can understand why. Kale is a super food—not only is it low in calories (only about 33 calories per cup), it also contains huge amounts of vitamins A, C, and K, plus calcium and fiber. All that nutrition is exactly what your body needs. This lemony salad pairs the crisp, tough kale leaves with creamy avocado to give you a super-healthy (and tasty) midday meal.

Makes 1 serving

1 avocado

2½ cups kale leaves

3 tablespoons Lemon Vinaigrette (recipe on page 130)

⅓ cup sliced red onion

1 quart-size Mason jar

Cut the avocado in half and discard the pit. Using a spoon, remove the avocado flesh from the outer skin; cut into ½-inch cubes and set aside.

Remove the center ribs from the kale leaves and cut them into 1½- to 2-inch pieces. Kale is best when lightly massaged to take away some of the toughness, so place the leaves in a bowl and gently rub them together with your hands to soften them. Be careful not to massage them *too* much, especially if you're planning to eat the salad toward the end of the coming week.

Layer the ingredients in the jar, starting with your dressing, then adding the onion and the kale. Finish with the diced avocado on top. Seal and refrigerate until ready to use.

TIPS

This salad is delicious made with mango, too! Cube a ½ cup of mango and add it on top of the kale. Top the salad with the avocado.

Avocados will last about 3 days in a Mason jar, but it will depend on the avocados' freshness. I don't recommend using super ripe avocados if you aren't planning on eating the salad the next day.

barley and kale salad

Greens and grains work beautifully together, and this salad is packed with both. The tomatoes, cucumber, and bell pepper add pops of acidity and crunch, but it's the kale and barley that really shine here.

Makes 1 serving

1 cup water

pinch of salt

½ cup quick-cooking barley, to make 1½ cups cooked barley

3 tablespoons White Wine Vinaigrette (recipe on page 132)

2½ tablespoons diced red onion

½ cup quartered English cucumber slices

½ cup halved cherry tomatoes

½ cup diced red bell pepper

2 cups roughly chopped kale, or enough to fill the rest of the jar*

1 quart-size Mason jar

Prepare the kale by removing the hard center ribs and chopping the leaves into 1½-inch pieces.

Pour the water into a saucepan over high heat, add a pinch of salt, and bring to a boil. Add the barley, reduce the temperature, and simmer, covered, for 10 to 12 minutes, or until the water has evaporated. Set aside and let cool while you prepare the rest of the salad.

Pour the vinaigrette into the Mason jar. Add layers of diced onion, cucumber, cherry tomatoes, 1 cup of the cooked barley, and red bell pepper. Fill the rest of the jar with the kale. Seal and refrigerate until ready to use.

greek salad with chickpeas

Spicing up a Greek salad with chickpeas is always a good idea. This tasty, greens-free salad is perfect when you're tired of eating leafy greens but still want to keep lunch healthy. You can't go wrong with feta cheese and olives, and the chickpeas help curb your appetite while providing your body with zinc and protein. This salad is filling and satisfying without being a huge portion. I think you'll love it!

Makes 1 serving

2 tablespoons Lemon Vinaigrette (recipe on page 130)

½ cup chickpeas, rinsed and drained

⅓ cup halved cherry tomatoes

⅓ cup quartered cucumber slices

2 tablespoons diced red onion

2 tablespoons pitted black olives, halved

2 ounces crumbled feta cheese

2 tablespoons chopped fresh parsley

1 pint-size Mason jar

Place the vinaigrette in the Mason jar and add the chickpeas. Next add layers of cherry tomatoes, cucumber, onion, olives, feta cheese, and parsley. Seal and refrigerate until you're ready to eat the salad.

mixed greens with white bean salad

I whip up this white bean salad when I need a light snack or dinner. With herbs, cannellini beans, lemon, and red wine vinegar, the salad goes perfectly with pita bread, but it's also terrific when added to a green salad. Beans and greens make a healthy meal that's packed with protein.

Makes 1 serving

2 tablespoons Red Wine Vinaigrette (recipe on page 130)
½ cup White Bean Salad (recipe follows)
½ cup quartered English cucumber slices
½ cup chopped vine-ripened tomatoes
2½ to 3 cups spring mix salad greens
1 quart-size Mason jar

Layer the ingredients in the Mason jar, starting with the vinaigrette and then adding the bean salad, followed by the cucumber and tomatoes. Fill the rest of the jar with the salad greens. Seal and refrigerate until ready to use.

white bean salad

Makes 2 half-pint servings

3 tablespoons chopped red onion
1 tablespoon olive oil
1 to 2 teaspoons red wine vinegar
1 tablespoon lemon juice
1 (15-ounce) can cannellini beans, rinsed and drained
3 tablespoons chopped fresh parsley
½ teaspoon chopped fresh rosemary
½ teaspoon chopped fresh thyme
salt and black pepper

Place the red onion in a bowl with the olive oil, vinegar, and lemon juice. Add the cannellini beans, parsley, rosemary, thyme, and salt and pepper to taste. Toss together to add to the Mason jar salad or enjoy on its own.

spinach, radish, and quinoa salad

While it may seem like a grain, quinoa is actually a seed—an awesome, nutrition-packed seed. Quinoa is a great source of protein, fiber, and iron, and its fluffy texture makes it a perfect addition to salads. Here I've included it in a spring salad along with spinach, radishes, and peas.

Makes 1 serving

¼ cup uncooked quinoa

½ cup water

2 to 3 tablespoons Blueberry Vinaigrette (recipe on page 132)

⅓ cup cucumber chunks

⅓ cup diced vine-ripened tomatoes

⅓ cup fresh peas (or substitute sugar snap peas)

½ cup thinly sliced radishes

2 cups spinach leaves

1 quart-size Mason jar

Rinse the quinoa thoroughly under running water. Place in a small saucepan with the water and bring to a boil over high heat. Reduce the heat to a simmer and cook, covered, for 15 minutes, until the water has been absorbed. Let the quinoa cool before adding it to the salad.

Layer the ingredients in the Mason jar, starting with the vinaigrette dressing and continuing with the cucumbers, tomatoes, peas, and radishes. Add the cooled quinoa and finish with the spinach greens. Seal and refrigerate until ready to use.

bulgur wheat salad

Bulgur wheat is an often-overlooked whole grain that works really well in this Mediterranean salad. This recipe makes a sizeable salad, perfect if you need to bring something to a dinner or are feeding several people. If you're making it just for yourself, you can halve the recipe and use a pint-size jar.

Makes 2 servings

½ cup uncooked bulgur wheat

1 cup boiling water

3 tablespoons Lemon Vinaigrette (recipe on page 130)

½ cup chickpeas, rinsed and drained

3 tablespoons chopped red onion

½ cup cubed English cucumber

½ cup diced red bell pepper

½ cup halved heirloom baby tomatoes

2 tablespoons chopped fresh dill

2 tablespoons chopped fresh parsley

2½ ounces crumbled feta cheese

1 quart-size Mason jar

Place the bulgur wheat in a Pyrex bowl and add the boiling water. Cover the bowl with plastic wrap and let sit for 20 minutes, or until the water is mostly absorbed. If there's water left in the bowl, drain the bulgur and set it aside to cool.

Pour the vinaigrette into the Mason jar. Layer the salad into the jar, starting with the chickpeas, red onion, cucumber, and red bell pepper. The next layer should be the bulgur, packed down. On top of the bulgur, layer the tomatoes, dill, and parsley. Finish with the feta cheese. Seal the jar and refrigerate until ready to use.

strawberry and goat cheese salad

This is one of my very favorite spring salads. You know spring has hit when you go to the farmers' market one weekend and, like magic, crate upon crate of strawberries have appeared at the stands. It's a glorious time, one you don't want to miss out on. When strawberry season hits, I try to consume strawberries at as many different meals as possible—not just for dessert!

There are no firm veggies to create a barrier between the dressing and the other ingredients in this salad. Instead, I suggest using parchment paper or plastic wrap to create a cup for the dressing at the top of your Mason jar (for instructions, see page 14). When you're ready to eat your salad, just dump the dressing into your bowl, empty the salad ingredients into the bowl, and toss it all together.

Makes 1 serving

⅔ cup strawberries, sliced

3 cups spinach leaves, divided

⅓ cup walnuts

1½ ounces crumbled goat cheese

2 to 3 tablespoons Balsamic Vinaigrette (page 131)

1 quart-size Mason jar

Place the strawberries in the bottom of the Mason jar, holding off on the salad dressing. Add 2 cups of the spinach, then the walnuts. The next layer is the remaining cup of spinach. Finish with the goat cheese.

Create a cup at the top of the jar with a piece of parchment paper or plastic wrap. Add your dressing and then twist on the lid over the parchment or plastic wrap. Refrigerate until ready to use.

asian greens salad

My favorite salad vendor at the farmers' market sometimes sells wasabi greens and an Asian salad mix, which gave me the idea for this salad. The spicy wasabi greens pair well with the sweet mandarin oranges and crunchy chow mein noodles.

Makes 1 serving

3 tablespoons Citrus-Soy Vinaigrette (recipe on page 133)

½ cup diced red bell pepper

½ cup mandarin oranges

2 cups Asian greens (such as mizuna or red and green mustard greens)

2 tablespoons chopped green onion, green tops removed

½ cup wasabi greens

½ cup alfalfa sprouts

3 tablespoons canned crispy chow mein noodles

1 quart-size Mason jar

Pour the vinaigrette into the Mason jar. Next add the red pepper as a barrier between the dressing and the following layer, the mandarin oranges. Now add the salad greens — first the Asian greens, then the green onions, wasabi greens, and sprouts. Top with the chow mein noodles, seal the jar, and refrigerate until ready to use.

cobb salad

The Cobb salad is said to be the creation of Robert Cobb, the owner of the Hollywood Brown Derby restaurant, back in the 1930s. The Cobb salad quickly became a signature dish at the restaurant, and it lives on at restaurants across the country—and in home kitchens, too!

Chopped salads are fantastic for lunch, because they are filling and filled with protein. All the different proteins make this Cobb salad especially pretty packed in a pint jar, but you can easily expand it into a quart jar by adding more romaine. You can grill a chicken breast to use in the salad or use leftover cooked chicken.

Makes 1 serving

1 egg

2 slices bacon

½ avocado

1½ tablespoons French Vinaigrette (recipe on page 130)*

¼ cup diced tomatoes

2 tablespoons chopped fresh parsley

1 tablespoon chopped chives

¼ cup chopped romaine, cut in 2-inch strips*

¼ cup cubed cooked chicken breast

1 ounce blue cheese

1 pint-size Mason jar*

To use a quart-size jar, increase the vinaigrette to 3 tablespoons and the romaine to 2 cups.

Place the egg in a small saucepan and cover with water. Bring to a boil over high heat and then immediately turn off the burner. Cover the pan and let sit for 11 minutes, then remove the egg using a slotted spoon and cool briefly in a cold-water bath. Peel and chop the egg; set aside.

In a small skillet over low to medium heat, cook the bacon until crispy. Drain the bacon grease, chop into small pieces, and set aside. Cube the avocado.

Place the vinaigrette in the Mason jar, then layer in the tomatoes, parsley and chives, chopped egg, romaine, avocado, and chicken. Crumble the blue cheese into the jar and add the bacon on top. Seal and refrigerate until ready to use.

pomegranate and pear salad

This salad never fails to put me in the fall spirit. Pears and blue cheese pair beautifully, but it's the tart pomegranate seeds that really make this salad special. You can buy pomegranates whole and break them down yourself or purchase just the seeds at most grocery stores.

Makes 1 serving

1 pear, cored and thinly sliced

3 cups spinach leaves, divided

½ cup pomegranate seeds

¼ cup roughly chopped pecans

2 ounces crumbled blue cheese

3 tablespoons Sherry Vinaigrette (recipe on page 131)

1 quart-size Mason jar

Place the pear slices in the bottom of the Mason jar. Layer 2 cups of the spinach on top of the pear, then add the pomegranate seeds, another ½ cup spinach, and the chopped pecans. Finish with the remaining ½ cup spinach and the blue cheese.

Make a small cup out of parchment paper at the top of the jar (see page 14) and pour in the vinaigrette dressing. Seal the jar and refrigerate until ready to use.

crispy prosciutto and butter lettuce

This salad hits all your tastes buds—it has light and summery notes with the corn and cherry tomatoes, and then has salty, earthy tones with the prosciutto and Gorgonzola. Butter lettuce is delicate and airy, so make sure not to crush it down too much when layering the salad.

Makes 1 serving

1 ear of corn, husk and silks removed

1 to 2 teaspoons olive oil

2 slices prosciutto

3 tablespoons Lemon Vinaigrette (recipe on page 130)

½ cup halved cherry tomatoes

2 cups butter lettuce, torn into 2-inch pieces

1 to 2 ounces crumbled Gorgonzola cheese

1 quart-size Mason jar

Pour enough water into a pot to cover the corn. Bring to a boil over high heat, add the corn, and boil for 5 minutes. Remove the corn from the water and let cool for a few minutes. Cut the kernels off the cob.

Heat the olive oil in a skillet over medium heat. Add the prosciutto and cook until it starts to shrink and become crispy, about 3 minutes. Remove from the heat and transfer to a paper towel to cool, then chop into small pieces.

To assemble the salad, pour the vinaigrette into the Mason jar, then add the tomatoes and layer on the corn kernels. Add the butter lettuce, making sure not to pack it too tightly—it crushes easily. Add the Gorgonzola and top the salad with the crispy prosciutto pieces. Seal the jar and refrigerate until ready to use.

fruit salad

Mason jars are a great way to keep fruit fresh, and quart jars are a great way to transport fruit salads to picnics. Put a little orange juice at the bottom of the jar and when you empty it out, the juice will help keep the fruit from turning brown as it sits in a bowl.

Makes 1 serving

1 orange

½ cup grapes

½ cup cubed mango*

1 kiwi fruit, sliced

½ cup blueberries

½ cup raspberries

¼ cup strawberries

1 quart-size Mason jar

* For mango-cubing directions, see the recipe for Curry Chicken Salad on page 85.

Squeeze the juice from half of the orange into the Mason jar. Cut the rest of the orange into bite-size pieces and add them to the jar. Halve the grapes. Layer the mango cubes and grapes on top of the orange. Add the kiwi fruit, then the blueberries, raspberries, and strawberries. Make sure the jar is full — the less air in the jar, the better the fruit will keep. Seal and refrigerate until ready to use.

guacamole salad

If you love guacamole as much as I do, you're always looking for an excuse to go out for Mexican food. Well, now you can have it any day of the week, guilt free! This salad is a deconstructed guacamole with salad greens. If you like a little more heat, spice up the vinaigrette with hot sauce, or add more jalapeños.

Makes 1 serving

3 tablespoons Lime Vinaigrette (recipe on page 131, with hot sauce, optional)

3 tablespoons chopped red onion

1 teaspoon finely diced jalapeño chile

1 tomato, diced

3 cups mesclun salad greens

1 tablespoon chopped fresh cilantro

1 avocado

1 cooked chicken breast half, cubed (optional)

1 quart-size Mason jar

Pour the vinaigrette into the Mason jar. Add the onion, followed by the jalapeño and diced tomato. Layer on the mesclun and then the cilantro.

Cut the avocado in half and discard the pit. Use a spoon to separate the avocado flesh from the peel. Cube the avocado and layer it on top of the salad greens. Seal the jar and refrigerate until ready to use. To include cubed chicken breast, add it to the jar in the morning on the day you're planning to eat the salad.

hearts of palm salad

White and a little crunchy, hearts of palm are a truly underappreciated vegetable. As the name describes, they are literally the center cores of certain types of palm trees. The taste is comparable to that of an artichoke, and hearts of palm are a good source of potassium and vitamin B6.

Makes 1 serving

4 asparagus stalks
1 to 2 tablespoons Lime Vinaigrette (recipe on page 131)
1 cup hearts of palm, sliced (from a jar or can)
½ cup halved cherry tomatoes
1 to 2 tablespoons chopped fresh parsley
black pepper
1 pint-size Mason jar

Bring a saucepan of salted water to a boil over high heat, add the asparagus, and cook for 2 minutes, until the asparagus is bright green and just cooked through. Remove from the pan and submerge in an ice-water bath for a minute to stop the cooking. Remove and trim off the bottom 1½ inches of each stalk. Cut the stalks into 1-inch pieces.

Add the vinaigrette to the Mason jar, followed by the hearts of palm, tomatoes, and cooked asparagus. Top with the parsley and some black pepper, to taste. Seal the jar and refrigerate until ready to use.

caesar salad

Caesar salad is very basic, but that doesn't mean it shouldn't be eaten out of a Mason jar! Bring this salad to work in a pint jar to complement a sandwich. Caesar dressing is usually made with egg yolks and anchovies; given these ingredients and the fact that the salad may sit in the fridge for a few days, I recommend using store-bought dressing.

Makes 1 serving

1½ cups chopped romaine lettuce

2 tablespoons shaved Parmigiano-Reggiano cheese

¼ cup croutons, store-bought or homemade

1 to 2 tablespoons prepared Caesar dressing

1 pint-size Mason jar

Place the romaine lettuce in the Mason jar. Add the cheese and top with the croutons. Make a parchment paper cup (see page 14) and add the Caesar dressing. Seal the jar over the parchment and refrigerate until ready to use.

Making Your Own Croutons

If you have bread that you need to use before it goes stale, homemade croutons are the perfect solution. Preheat your oven to 375°F. Rip the bread into 1-inch pieces, about the size of croutons, until you have about ½ cup. In a small bowl, mix the bread pieces with 2 tablespoons olive oil and season with salt, pepper, and a little garlic powder to taste. Spread onto a rimmed baking sheet and bake for about 15 minutes, or until crispy and golden. Remove from the oven and let cool.

apple and frisée salad

When summer begins to turn into fall, apples arrive at the farmers' markets and you know it's time for some apple-based salads. Apple and frisée salad is simple to make but shouldn't be underestimated, and it's a great way to get your fill of freshly harvested apples while you can. The apples won't turn brown as long as you pack everything tightly so there isn't too much air in the jar.

Makes 1 serving

1 Gala or Honeycrisp apple

2½ cups chopped frisée salad greens, cut in 2-inch pieces, divided

1½ tablespoons shallots, chopped

¼ cup chopped walnuts

2 ounces crumbled goat cheese

3 tablespoons Apple Cider Vinaigrette with Honey (recipe on page 132)

1 quart-size Mason jar

Core the apple and slice it into thin pieces. Place the apple slices in the bottom of the Mason jar and top with a cup of the frisée, then layer on the shallots, another cup of frisée, the walnuts, and the rest of the frisée. Finish with the goat cheese. Make a parchment paper cup on top for the vinaigrette (see page 14), or carry it separately in a small container. Seal the jar and refrigerate until ready to use.

spinach, blueberry, and blue cheese salad

Fruit and cheese go incredibly well together, and this salad is no exception. Blueberries and blue cheese are the stars of the show in this sweet and salty summer salad. The strength of their flavors elevates a simple spinach salad to something complex and biting—perfect for lunch or as part of a summer barbecue.

Makes 1 serving

½ cup blueberries

3 cups spinach leaves, divided

¼ cup shaved or sliced almonds

2 ounces crumbled blue cheese

3 tablespoons Red Wine Vinaigrette (recipe on page 130)

1 quart-size Mason jar

Place the blueberries in the bottom of the Mason jar. Next make layers of 2 cups spinach, the almonds, and the remaining 1 cup spinach. The final layer should be the blue cheese.

On top of the blue cheese, make a parchment paper cup (see page 14) and pour in the Red Wine Vinaigrette. Seal the jar and refrigerate until you're ready to eat the salad.

TIP

If you're going to eat this salad on the same day you make it, you can put the dressing in the bottom of the jar and eliminate the parchment paper cup. Otherwise, the salad will last longer if the blueberries don't sit in the dressing.

blt panzanella

Panzanella is a Tuscan peasant salad made with tomatoes, basil, vinaigrette, and stale bread. Panzanella is perfect when you want to make use of a baguette you just couldn't finish the night before. Here I decided to spice things up by deconstructing one of my favorite simple sandwiches, the BLT, and remaking it in panzanella form.

Makes 1 serving

3 strips bacon
2 to 3 tablespoons Lemon Vinaigrette (recipe on page 130)
½ cup halved cherry tomatoes or diced heirloom tomatoes
⅓ cup mesclun salad mix
⅓ cup Tuscan bread cubes or baguette*
1 pint-size Mason jar
* Cut or tear a piece of day-old bread into 1-inch chunks.

In a skillet over low to medium heat, cook the bacon until crispy. Drain on a paper towel, chop into small pieces, and set aside.

Pour the vinaigrette into the Mason jar. Add the tomatoes and then the greens. Place the bread pieces directly on top of the greens, or separate them with a piece of parchment paper if you prefer to keep the bread from absorbing any moisture. Seal the jar and refrigerate. When it's time to eat the salad, mix everything together in a bowl and let sit for a few minutes so the bread softens and absorbs some of the dressing.

more lunch ideas

The dishes in this chapter are fantastic at dinnertime, but they can just as easily go into Mason jars so that you can grab a perfectly portioned meal whenever you need it. These soups, pastas, risottos, and rice dishes make use of the same produce as the salads in this book, ensuring that you'll be able to eat a variety of light and healthy meals.

tortellini with basil pesto, cherry tomatoes, and mozzarella

Every summer I grow basil plants and harvest them to make big batches of pesto. If you don't have the space to grow your own plants, keep an eye out at farmers' markets or local stores during the summer, when basil prices are low. This caprese-style salad takes very little time to make and keeps well in the refrigerator, either in layers or mixed together, so you can feel free to make it days in advance. This recipe is perfect for large gatherings; cut the recipe in half for a single serving to bring to the office.

Makes 2 servings

2 cups uncooked fresh cheese tortellini

1 tablespoon olive oil (if using a Mason jar)

2 tablespoons Basil Pesto (recipe follows)

1 tablespoon thinly sliced red onion

1 cup cherry tomatoes, halved

¼ cup halved mozzarella balls

1 quart-size Mason jar (optional)

Cook the tortellini according to the package directions; drain and transfer to a bowl. If you're planning to layer your salad in a jar, mix in the olive oil to keep the tortellini from sticking together.

To layer the salad, start with the pesto and then add the onion, tomatoes, mozzarella, and tortellini. Or, simply mix the remaining ingredients with the tortellini in the bowl. Seal the jar or cover the bowl; refrigerate until ready to use.

This recipe can be eaten warm or cold.

basil pesto

Makes 4 servings

¼ cup plus 1 tablespoon olive oil, divided

¼ cup pine nuts

4 cups tightly packed basil leaves

½ cup grated Parmigiano-Reggiano cheese

¼ **teaspoon salt**

¼ **teaspoon black pepper**

In a small skillet, heat 1 tablespoon olive oil over medium heat. Add the pine nuts and toast, stirring frequently, until golden brown, about 3 minutes.

In a blender or food processor, combine the basil, ¼ cup olive oil, cheese, toasted pine nuts, salt, and pepper. Blend until the ingredients come together smoothly.

TIP

If you have a lot of basil on your hands, you can make a big batch of pesto and freeze it to use later. Just pour the pesto into an ice cube tray and freeze. Once the pesto is frozen, you can remove it from the ice cube tray and store it in a zip-top plastic bag in the freezer. When you want pesto for your salad, drop frozen pesto into the pasta pot after you've drained it and it will quickly defrost.

pasta alla nerano

I tried this native Amalfi Coast staple the first time I visited Sorrento in southern Italy, and I've been trying to replicate it ever since. The strength of this dish is its simplicity: pasta, zucchini, basil, olive oil, and Parmigiano cheese are all you need to make a light and fresh pasta that tastes just as delicious the next day.

Makes 4 servings

½ cup olive oil

4 zucchini, thinly sliced

⅓ cup julienne-cut basil leaves (the more the better, really)

salt and black pepper

1 pound package spaghetti

½ cup grated Parmigiano-Reggiano cheese, plus more for serving

4 pint-size Mason jars

Heat the olive oil in a skillet over medium heat. Add the zucchini and sauté for 5 minutes, until it starts to soften. Add the basil, season with salt and freshly ground black pepper to taste, and cook for 2 to 3 more minutes.

Follow the package directions to cook the spaghetti al dente. Drain and add to the skillet with the zucchini mixture. Stir in the ½ cup grated cheese and more pepper, if desired. Serve at once, adding more grated cheese, or let cool and divide the pasta among your Mason jars. Seal and refrigerate until ready to use. To bring more cheese to work with you, use some parchment paper to keep it separate from the pasta. Place the pasta in a bowl and reheat before eating.

orecchiette and broccoli rabe

Broccoli rabe has a bitter, peppery taste that I find irresistible. The strength of its flavor means that it can stand alone with just a little bit of garlic and red pepper flakes for seasoning. Add some orecchiette and you have an awesome sauceless pasta that's great either for dinner or for lunch for days to come.

Makes 4 servings

¼ cup olive oil

2 garlic cloves, chopped

¼ teaspoon red pepper flakes

1 bunch broccoli rabe

2 cups uncooked orecchiette

¼ cup white wine

Parmigiano-Reggiano cheese, grated for serving

4 pint-size Mason jars

Heat the olive oil in a large skillet over medium heat. Add the garlic and red pepper flakes and cook, stirring, until the garlic is golden, about a minute. Remove the pan from the heat and set aside.

Bring a pot of salted water to a boil over high heat. While the water is heating, trim about 3 inches off the broccoli rabe stems. Clean the broccoli rabe thoroughly in cold water to remove any grit from between the leaves. Roughly chop into quarters. Add to the boiling water and cook for about 3 minutes, until bright green. Transfer to a bowl and set aside, but leave the water in the pot for cooking the pasta. Add the orecchiette to the boiling water and cook until al dente, around 10 minutes.

Meanwhile, return the skillet with the garlic to the stove over medium heat and stir in the broccoli rabe. Drain the cooked orecchiette and add it to the skillet. Pour in the white wine and cook until the wine cooks off.

To serve, grate Parmigiano-Reggiano over the pasta. Eat at once, or let cool and transfer to Mason jars for lunch. When you're ready to eat, transfer the orecchiette to a bowl to reheat.

curry chicken salad

Chicken salad is a great way to use leftovers from a chicken you've roasted for dinner. Otherwise, you can easily pick up a rotisserie chicken at your grocery store to make this tasty salad for the coming week. Tangy mango and mildly spicy curry give this recipe a little extra kick. Eat the salad by itself, or bring bread to make a great sandwich.

Makes about 2 servings

½ mango, cubed

1 roast chicken, about 1½ cups cubed chicken

½ teaspoon curry powder

5 tablespoons mayonnaise

1 stalk celery, thinly sliced

2½ tablespoons diced red onion

salt and black pepper

sandwich bread (optional)

2 half-pint Mason jars

Cutting a Mango

A mango has a large, flat seed that you need to cut around. Hold the mango upright and slice off one side, cutting almost up against the pit (roughly a third of the way into the mango). Do the same with the other side. If flesh is left around the seed, cut it off; discard the seed. To make cubes, take a mango piece and make diagonal slices into the flesh, trying not to cut all the way through the skin. Then make diagonal slices in the other direction, creating squares. Slide your knife under the mango flesh to cut off the cubed mango.

In a bowl, combine the cubed mango, cubed chicken, curry powder, mayonnaise, celery, and red onion. Season with salt and pepper to taste.

Spoon the salad into the Mason jar, seal, and refrigerate until ready to use. To make a chicken salad sandwich, bring 2 slices of bread to work in a zip-top plastic bag. If you have access to a toaster there, all the better!

potato salad

This potato salad is perfect for bringing to a picnic in a big jar, but that shouldn't stop you from also bringing it to work as an afternoon snack or as a side for a sandwich. If you prefer a little more bite, try adding curry powder or paprika to give it a bit of a kick.

Makes 4 servings

3 pounds thin-skinned red and white potatoes

½ cup mayonnaise

2 teaspoons lemon juice

½ cup roughly chopped fresh parsley

2 tablespoons country-style Dijon mustard

3 tablespoons chopped chives

½ cup thinly sliced celery (about 2 stalks)

salt and black pepper

4 pint-size or 2 quart-size Mason jars

Place the potatoes in a pot of salted water, making sure the water covers them completely. Bring the water to a boil over high heat, then reduce the heat and simmer for 15 to 20 minutes, until the potatoes are tender when pierced with a fork. Drain and set aside to cool.

In a small bowl, mix together the mayonnaise, lemon juice, parsley, mustard, and chives. Set aside.

Once the potatoes have cooled, quarter them and place in a bowl along with the celery. Add the mayonnaise mixture and season to taste with salt and pepper. Toss everything together to combine. Spoon the potato salad into the Mason jars, seal, and refrigerate until ready to use.

penne all'amatriciana

Here's one of my favorite pasta sauces of all time—all'amatriciana sauce, a Roman classic. Pancetta, an Italian meat similar to unsmoked bacon, and onion elevate a traditional tomato sauce to something much more special.

While this sauce is typically served over bucatini pasta, penne is easier to fit into a Mason jar. Also, the hole that runs through the center of bucatini makes it easy to spray your shirt with sauce—a dangerous possibility if you're eating at work!

Makes 4 servings

4 tablespoons olive oil, divided

1 yellow onion, diced

2 garlic cloves, minced

6 to 8 ounces pancetta, chopped

1 teaspoon red pepper flakes

1 (28-ounce) can whole peeled tomatoes

1 pound box penne pasta

Parmigiano-Reggiano cheese, grated for serving

4 pint-size Mason jars

Heat 3 tablespoons olive oil in a skillet over medium heat. Add the onion and cook until translucent. Next add the garlic, pancetta, and red pepper flakes and cook until the pancetta starts to crisp and lightly brown, 4 to 5 minutes.

While the pancetta mixture is cooking, purée the tomatoes in a blender, being careful not to over-liquefy them. Add to the pancetta, increase the heat to high, and bring to a boil, then reduce the heat to a simmer and cook, covered, for 15 minutes.

As the sauce simmers, follow the package directions to cook the penne al dente. Drain the pasta and, if you'll be placing it in a Mason jar, stir in the remaining 1 tablespoon olive oil to keep it from sticking together.

Add about ¾ cup of sauce to each of the Mason jars and then fill the jars the rest of the way with penne (you should have about 1½ cups of penne). Add some grated Parmigiano-Reggiano cheese on top and seal the jars. Store in the refrigerator until ready to use. When ready to eat, transfer to a bowl to reheat.

TIP

This recipe makes quite a lot of sauce. If you're cooking for a single person, you can place leftover sauce in a Mason jar and freeze it. The frozen sauce will be good for 6 months.

orzo pasta salad

Sun-dried tomatoes are Roma plum tomatoes that, even today, are dried in the sun until they lose most of their water content. Adding sun-dried tomatoes to dishes can be tricky because of their distinct, concentrated flavor. Here the taste is balanced by plain orzo and leafy spinach greens.

Makes 1 serving

1 cup uncooked orzo

½ tablespoon olive oil

2 tablespoons Red Wine Vinaigrette (recipe on page 130)

1 tablespoon chopped red onion

1 cup spinach leaves

¼ cup sliced sun-dried tomatoes, cut into thin strips

1 to 2 ounces crumbled feta cheese

1 pint-size Mason jar

Following the package directions, cook the orzo until al dente, about 10 minutes. Drain, transfer to a bowl, and toss with the olive oil to keep it from sticking together.

Add the vinaigrette and chopped onion to the Mason jar. Layer the cooked orzo, spinach, and sun-dried tomatoes in the jar and top with the feta cheese. Seal and refrigerate until ready to use. Eat at room temperature or reheated.

chicken and vegetable stir-fry

If you're like me, you often find yourself looking for ways to use a bunch of produce all at once. Stir-fries provide an easy way to do just that, and they're super satisfying as well. Cook your veggies with some chicken, add rice, and you're good to go. Not only will you have a great meal, but this quick dinner tastes just as good the next day for lunch.

Makes 4 to 6 servings

2 tablespoons soy sauce

2 tablespoons unseasoned rice wine vinegar

2 tablespoons honey

1 teaspoon red pepper flakes

1 pound chicken breasts

3 tablespoons vegetable oil, divided

1 red bell pepper, sliced

1 yellow bell pepper, sliced

½ yellow onion, sliced

2 garlic cloves, chopped

1½ cups sugar snap peas

1 tablespoon cornstarch

1 tablespoon water

cooked rice, for serving

4 to 6 pint-size Mason jars

In a small bowl, combine the soy sauce, rice wine vinegar, honey, and red pepper flakes. Set aside. Slice the chicken breasts lengthwise into 1-inch-wide strips.

Heat 2 tablespoons of the oil in a wok or large skillet over medium-high heat. Add the bell peppers, onion, and garlic and cook, stirring, until the peppers and onion start to soften, about 3 minutes. Transfer the vegetables to a plate.

Return the wok or skillet to the heat and add the remaining 1 tablespoon oil. Add the chicken and cook over high heat, stirring, until it is opaque and starting to cook through, about 4 minutes. At this point, return the peppers and onion to the wok or skillet and add the snap peas and soy-honey mixture.

In a small bowl, whisk together the cornstarch and water. Add to the wok or skillet, bring everything to a boil, and simmer until the sauce thickens and reduces, 3 to 4 minutes. Remove the stir-fry from the stove and serve at once over rice, or let cool to put into Mason jars. For lunch on the go, fill the bottom half of a pint-size jar with stir-fry and the top half with cooked rice. Seal the jar and refrigerate. When ready to eat, just empty the jar onto a plate and reheat in the microwave oven.

fried rice

Fried rice is an easy dish to prepare once you have the basic seasonings on hand. Then, whenever you have leftover rice from a meal you've made at home, you'll be able to create an entirely different and flavorful lunch. Fried rice is also an easy way to work vegetables into your diet; pretty much any produce you have in your fridge can be added to fried rice.

Makes 4 servings

1 teaspoon tomato paste

1 tablespoon light brown sugar

2 garlic cloves, minced

2 chili peppers or jalapeño chiles, roughly chopped

2 tablespoons water

2 cups chopped baby bok choy, broccoli florets, or broccoli rabe

1 (8-ounce) package sliced cremini mushrooms

¼ cup peanut oil, divided

5 cups cooked rice (preferably leftovers)

5 tablespoons soy sauce

salt and black pepper

4 pint-size Mason jars

Place the tomato paste, brown sugar, garlic, and jalapeños in the bowl of a food processor with the water. Purée until the consistency is smooth.

In a skillet, toss the bok choy (or other vegetables) and mushrooms lightly in 1 tablespoon of peanut oil and sauté over medium heat for about 5 minutes, stirring frequently. The vegetables will cook more when they are added to the rice later, so there's no need to overdo it.

> **TIP**
> It's easy to add a protein to this meal. Just cut up cooked chicken, steak, or pork and place on top of the fried rice in the morning of the day you'll be eating it.

In a separate skillet or wok, heat the rest of the peanut oil over medium-high heat. Add the puréed seasoning mixture and cook until fragrant, stirring, 2 to 3 minutes. Add the rice and stir, breaking up any clumps. Cook until heated through, 7 to 10 minutes. While continuing to stir, add the soy sauce and cook until evenly distributed, 30 seconds more. Season to taste with salt and pepper, scoop your vegetable mixture onto the rice, and stir to combine.

Enjoy some of your fried rice at once, or let it cool to pack in Mason jars. Carefully spoon it into the jars, seal, and refrigerate. For delicious meals throughout the week, just heat the fried rice in the microwave oven.

pasta e fagioli

Pasta e fagioli originated in Italy as a peasant dish because it consisted of very basic and inexpensive ingredients. My great aunt, Zia Ida, makes an amazing pasta e fagioli, so I sought out her expertise to come up with this recipe. While the soup was traditionally made without meat (because meat was expensive), I've added a bit of pancetta here. If you're a vegetarian, just leave out the pancetta and use a vegetable bouillon cube instead of beef. The soup will still be fantastic.

Makes 6 servings

2 tablespoons olive oil

3 ounces pancetta, chopped (optional)

½ yellow onion, chopped

2 garlic cloves, finely diced

1 carrot, peeled and finely diced

1 celery stalk, finely diced

½ teaspoon rosemary, finely chopped

½ teaspoon thyme, finely chopped

5 cups water

1 beef bouillon cube

1 (28-ounce) can diced tomatoes

1¼ cups uncooked ditalini pasta

1 (15-ounce) can cannellini or borlotti beans, rinsed and drained

salt and black pepper

½ cup chopped fresh parsley

Parmigiano-Reggiano cheese, grated for serving

6 pint-size Mason jars

In a medium saucepan, heat the olive oil over medium heat. Add the chopped pancetta to the hot oil, if using. Cook until the pancetta is cooked through and about to brown, then add the onion, garlic, carrot, celery, rosemary, and thyme. Season with black pepper and salt and cook until the vegetables are softened and starting to brown.

While the vegetables and pancetta are cooking, bring the water to a boil in a saucepan over high heat and add the bouillon cube and stir to dissolve it. Remove from the heat and set aside. Lightly purée the tomatoes in a blender. Add the tomatoes and the bouillon to the softened vegetables and bring to a boil over high heat, then reduce the heat to medium and cook for 10 more minutes.

Bring the soup back to a boil and add the pasta and the beans. Cook until the pasta is al dente, 10 to 11 minutes, stirring often. Stir in the parsley, add some grated cheese on top, and enjoy! Or let cool and pour into Mason jars, seal, and refrigerate until ready to use. Reheat in the microwave making sure to stir it at least once while reheating.

roasted cauliflower with parmesan cheese

I know what you're thinking: cauliflower, really? But stay with me here, I promise that it's good! Lemon, olive oil, garlic, and Parmesan cheese are magical, transforming cauliflower into a tasty snack or lunch that you'll crave.

Makes about 3 servings

1 head cauliflower

2 medium garlic cloves

½ small yellow onion, cut lengthwise into ¼-inch slices

3 sprigs fresh thyme

2 tablespoons olive oil

juice from ½ lemon

salt and black pepper

½ cup grated Parmigiano-Reggiano cheese

3 pint-size Mason jars

Preheat your oven to 425°F. Cut the cauliflower into individual florets, then cut each floret in half. Slice the garlic cloves lengthwise into thirds. Toss the cauliflower and garlic in a bowl with the onion, thyme, olive oil, lemon juice, and salt and pepper to taste.

Transfer the vegetable mixture to a baking dish and roast for 35 minutes, turning the vegetables over halfway through. Remove from the oven, sprinkle on the cheese, and stir. Return the dish to the oven for an additional 10 minutes, then remove and let cool. Seal in a Mason jar and refrigerate for a healthy and delicious work lunch or snack. Reheat in a microwave before eating.

potatoes and peppers

I love recipes like this that work well either as side dishes or as meals on their own—and take very little effort to pull together. Serve this for dinner along with grilled chicken and a salad, or take it to work to eat with a bit of crusty bread on the side. It's spicy, sweet, satisfying, and easy.

Makes 2 to 3 servings

24 small sweet peppers, around 1 pound

15 golden potatoes, quartered

1 teaspoon dried parsley

1 teaspoon dried garlic flakes

1 teaspoon red pepper flakes, or to taste

¼ cup olive oil, enough to lightly coat everything

salt and black pepper

2 or 3 pint-size Mason jars

Preheat your oven to 375°F. Cut the peppers into ½-inch-wide strips, removing any seeds. Place in a baking dish along with the potatoes.

In a small bowl, mix together the parsley, garlic, red pepper, and a sprinkling of salt. Distribute the mixed spices over the peppers and potatoes, adding more red pepper if you like it spicier. Add the olive oil and a little black pepper and mix everything together.

Bake for 45 minutes, turning the potatoes and peppers after about 20 minutes so they cook evenly. Remove from the oven, let cool, and transfer to Mason jars. Seal and refrigerate to take to work during the coming week. Reheat in a bowl in the microwave or eat at room temperature.

TIP

Grocery stores often sell small sweet peppers in packages. If there are packages at your store, just use one package for this recipe and forgo counting the peppers.

egg salad

Egg salad is a great lunch option because it takes surprisingly few ingredients to make and they are usually ingredients you already have in your fridge and spice cabinet. Other than boiling the eggs, this salad takes only minutes to make but it is tasty and filling. Try adding a little bit of cayenne pepper if you want to spice it up. Egg salad tastes great on its own, but is truly outstanding as a sandwich. Just bring some bread to work with you along with your Mason jar of egg salad, and put together a tasty sandwich with minimal effort.

Makes 2 servings

4 extra large hard boiled eggs, coarsely chopped
1 stalk celery, finely chopped
¼ red onion, diced
1½ to 2 tablespoons mayonnaise
1 teaspoon Dijon mustard
½ teaspoon ground cumin
dash of cayenne pepper (optional)
salt and black pepper
bread for sandwiches
2 half-pint Mason jars

Place the eggs in a small saucepan, adding water to cover. Bring the water to a boil over high heat, then remove from the heat and cover the pan. Let the eggs sit, covered, for about 11 minutes. Remove with a slotted spoon and place in a cold-water bath for about a minute.

While the eggs cook, finely chop the celery and dice the red onion. Peel the hard-cooked eggs and coarsely chop them. Place in a bowl with the onion and celery, then add the mayonnaise, mustard, cumin, and cayenne pepper, if using. Mix together and season to taste with salt and pepper.

Transfer the egg salad to the Mason jars, seal, and refrigerate. Bring a jar to work along with a couple of slices bread in a zip-top plastic bag.

spiced couscous

This couscous has earthy flavor tones that are tasty any time of the year but especially good when it starts to get cool. The cinnamon and raisins add sweet notes, balanced by the toasted pine nuts. Preparing the recipe takes 10 minutes tops. It's great served with grilled chicken, tofu, or vegetables.

Makes 4 servings

1 tablespoon butter

¾ teaspoon ground allspice

¾ teaspoon dried cilantro

¾ teaspoon ground cinnamon

¾ teaspoon ground cumin

2 teaspoons light brown sugar

2 cups vegetable broth

1½ cups instant couscous

½ cup pine nuts

½ cup raisins

½ cup chopped fresh parsley

salt and black pepper

4 pint-size Mason jars

Melt the butter in a saucepan over medium heat. Add the allspice, dried cilantro, cinnamon, cumin, and brown sugar. Stir for 1 minute to combine. Pour in the vegetable broth, increase the heat to bring to a boil and stir in the couscous. The moment you add the couscous, remove the pan from the heat and cover it. Let stand for 5 minutes.

While the couscous is resting, heat a small skillet over low heat. Add the pine nuts and lightly toast until golden, stirring frequently, for about 3 minutes.

Fluff the couscous with a spoon and stir in the raisins, pine nuts, and parsley. Season with salt and pepper to taste. To pack this for lunch, place 1 cup couscous in each Mason jar. Seal and refrigerate. On the day you're planning to eat the couscous, you can add grilled chicken or tofu on top. When you're ready to eat lunch, transfer to a plate and reheat.

gazpacho

What's better than a cold soup in the heat of the summer? This recipe is easy to turn to when tomatoes are in abundance.

Spanish cooking is all about using what you have and not being wasteful. So if you buy too many tomatoes, add more to the soup! Have a day-old baguette lying around? Perfect. Add it to the soup. Don't get too worried about the exact quantities —just add more of each ingredient until it tastes the way you want it to. This recipe comes to you directly from Spain; a Spanish friend visiting from Washington, DC, made an incredible gazpacho, so I asked for her advice.

Makes 4 servings, about 2 quarts

10 plum tomatoes

1 English cucumber, peeled

1 large red bell pepper

1 garlic clove

½ sweet white onion

⅓ baguette, torn into pieces

¼ cup white wine vinegar

½ cup olive oil, preferably Spanish

⅓ cup water

7 to 10 fresh parsley sprigs

½ jalapeño chile, seeded

salt and black pepper

4 pint-size Mason jars

Quarter the tomatoes, peel and quarter the cucumber, and cut into ¼-inch pieces. Seed the bell pepper and roughly dice it into ¼-inch pieces. Place in a food processor or blender along with the rest of the ingredients, including a dash of pepper and salt. Blend, then taste and season with more salt and pepper if necessary. Pour into Mason jars, seal, and refrigerate. At work, serve the soup straight out of the fridge, accompanied by bread.

chicken tortilla soup

I was first introduced to tortilla soup while visiting my father in New Mexico, when he was living in Los Alamos for a work assignment. I've loved it ever since. Chicken tortilla soup is perfectly balanced: you have protein, delicious vegetables, some carbs, and a whole lot of spice. What more could you ask for?

You can cook your chicken the day you make the soup, but if you're trying to save time, I recommend using leftovers or buying a rotisserie chicken from the grocery store.

Makes 6 servings

4 tablespoons olive oil, divided

½ yellow onion, chopped

1 carrot, peeled and finely diced

1 stalk celery, finely diced

2 garlic cloves, minced

½ jalapeño chile, finely diced

½ teaspoon cayenne pepper

2 teaspoons chili powder

1 teaspoon ground cumin

¼ teaspoon dried oregano

6 cups low-sodium chicken broth

1 (28-ounce) can diced tomatoes

10 corn tortillas

½ cup chopped fresh cilantro, plus cilantro sprigs for garnish

1 (15-ounce) can black beans, rinsed and drained

3 cups corn kernels, fresh or frozen

3 cooked chicken breast halves, shredded, about 1½ to 2 cups*

salt and black pepper

Monterey Jack cheese, grated for serving

1 lime, cut into 6 wedges

6 pint-size Mason jars

* Use 2 forks to shred the chicken.

Heat 3 tablespoons of the olive oil in a large pot over medium heat. Add the chopped onion and cook, stirring frequently, until it starts to soften. Add the carrot, celery, garlic, and jalapeño. Cook for an additional 3 minutes, or until the vegetables soften. Add the cayenne, chili powder, cumin, and oregano and stir for another minute.

Pour in the chicken broth and the diced tomatoes and bring to a boil. Cut 4 corn tortillas into ½-inch-wide strips and add to the soup along with the chopped cilantro. Lower the heat and simmer the soup, covered, until the tortillas disintegrate and the soup has thickened, about 30 minutes, stirring periodically. Then add the black beans, corn, and shredded chicken. Simmer for another 10 minutes.

While the soup simmers, preheat your oven to 375°F. Cut a few tortillas into ¼-inch-wide strips and toss them in a bowl with the remaining 1 tablespoon olive oil and a sprinkling of salt and pepper. Spread on a rimmed baking sheet and bake until golden and crispy, about 10 minutes. Let cool.

Serve the soup in bowls, topped with the crisp tortilla strips and grated Monterey Jack cheese; squeeze a lime wedge into each bowl. Or let the soup cool and pour it into Mason jars. Place some tortilla strips, cilantro, cheese, and a lime wedge in a parchment paper cup at the top of each jar (see page 14) to add after you've heated the soup. Seal the jars and refrigerate until ready to use. When ready to eat, heat the soup in the jar or transfer to a bowl.

curried butternut squash

Sometimes I'm not in the mood for a cold salad but want a warm vegetable dish instead. Here's the perfect solution — a hot dish with vegetables, legumes, and a little spice to make it special. Lime juice should be squeezed over the dish before you eat it, so be sure to tuck in a lime wedge at the top of the jar.

Makes 3 servings

1 (20-ounce) package fresh butternut squash

1 shallot, diced

3 tablespoons olive oil, divided

1½ teaspoons curry powder

salt and black pepper

½ cup uncooked lentils

1 cup water, or more as needed

½ cup roughly chopped walnuts

3 tablespoons chopped fresh cilantro

1 lime, quartered

3 pint-size Mason jars

Amount per jar:

1 cup curried butternut squash

½ cup cooked lentils

1½ tablespoons cilantro

2 to 3 tablespoons chopped walnuts

1 lime quarter

Preheat your oven to 420°F. Cut the squash into 1-inch cubes and place in a baking dish with the shallot, 2 tablespoons olive oil, curry powder, and a sprinkling of salt and pepper. Stir to combine. Bake for 30 minutes, or until the squash is tender when pierced. Toss occasionally to make sure the squash cooks evenly. Remove from the oven and let cool.

While the squash is cooking, put the lentils and water in a saucepan and bring to a low boil over medium to high heat. Reduce the heat and simmer the lentils for 20 minutes, or until tender. If needed, add a little more water while they cook. Once the lentils are tender, drain them, salt lightly, and set aside to cool.

Heat the remaining 1 tablespoon olive oil in a small skillet over medium heat. Add the walnuts and lightly toast them in the pan, stirring frequently for 3 to 4 minutes.

When the cooked ingredients have cooled, you can begin filling the Mason jars. Start each jar with 1 cup of squash and then add ½ cup lentils, 1½ tablespoons cilantro, and 2 to 3 tablespoons toasted walnuts. Before sealing the jar, place a lime quarter on top. When it's time to eat, remove the lime and empty everything else into a bowl. Stir together and heat in a microwave oven. Squeeze the lime over the hot food and enjoy.

chili

On cold days in fall or winter, sometimes you need a hearty soup to warm you up. This is a standard chili and a great base from which to start if you want to add more vegetables and spices. You can heat it in the microwave right in your Mason jar, no bowl necessary—just make sure to take off the top first!

Makes 4 servings

2 tablespoons olive oil

1 yellow onion, chopped

1 pound ground beef

2 garlic cloves, minced

1 teaspoon ground cumin

1 teaspoon dried thyme

½ teaspoon cayenne pepper

2 teaspoons chili powder

6 ounces tomato paste

1 (28-ounce) can diced tomatoes

1 (15-ounce) can kidney beans, rinsed and drained

1 green bell pepper, chopped

1 (8-ounce) package cremini mushrooms, sliced

grated Cheddar cheese, for serving (optional)

4 pint-size Mason jars

Heat 2 tablespoons olive oil in a large pot over medium heat. Add the onion and cook until it begins to soften. Add the ground beef and garlic, using a spoon to break apart the ground beef. Cook until the meat is browned. Add the spices—cumin, thyme, cayenne, and chili powder—and the tomato paste. Stir together and cook for another minute.

Add the diced tomatoes and kidney beans. Bring to a boil over high heat, then reduce the heat and simmer, covered, for 30 minutes. Add the bell pepper and mushrooms and simmer for an additional 15 to 30 minutes.

Let the chili cool and then spoon it into Mason jars. If you want to add Cheddar cheese, use parchment paper (see page 14) to keep it separate from the chili. Seal the jars and refrigerate until you're ready to heat and eat.

ratatouille

At some point during the heat of summer I'll go to the farmers' market and discover that overnight (or over a week), an absolute abundance of vegetables has appeared at all the stands—big purple eggplants, piles of zucchini, and tons of tomatoes. This is the moment when I know that summer has truly arrived.

Ratatouille is a dish that puts summer vegetables front and center. It takes a little time to make, and it isn't necessarily the most beautiful dish to look at, but ratatouille tastes exquisite! Bring it to work to eat either hot or at room temperature, with some bread on the side, or serve it at home over pasta.

Makes 4 servings

1 medium eggplant, cubed
salt
1 small to medium zucchini
1 yellow onion
1 green bell pepper
1 large tomato
2 garlic cloves, diced
red pepper flakes (optional)
3 basil leaves, cut into thin strips
2 tablespoons olive oil
4 pint-size Mason jars

Peel the eggplant and cut it into 1-inch cubes. Place the cubes on a paper towel–covered plate, then sprinkle with salt to draw out excess moisture. Let sit for 30 minutes and then pat the eggplant pieces dry.

> **TIP**
>
> If you want to eat your ratatouille over pasta for lunch, fill a pint jar halfway with ratatouille and the rest of the way with cooked penne pasta that has been tossed with a little olive oil to keep it from sticking together.

Meanwhile, cut the zucchini into 1-inch cubes, roughly dice the onion, and cut the pepper into strips. Cut the tomato into eighths.

Once the eggplant is ready, heat the olive oil in a large saucepan at medium heat. Add the eggplant, onion, bell pepper, garlic, and red pepper flakes, if using. Cook until the vegetables soften, about 10 minutes, stirring occasionally. Add the tomato wedges and basil and simmer, uncovered, for 30 minutes.

Remove from the heat and serve hot, or let cool and transfer to Mason jars for lunch. Seal the jars and refrigerate until ready to use. Reheat before eating.

asparagus risotto

A lot of fuss is made about the difficulty of making risotto, but I can tell you from experience that that's complete nonsense. Risotto is easy as long as you have a little time and patience. And once you know how to make one kind of risotto, you pretty much can make any version you want. They are all formed the same way—by slowly adding broth to rice. The only real changes are the extra ingredients you add to change the flavor profile.

The real difficulty with risotto is that it requires arm strength! You have to stir continually or it won't turn out right. But as long as you know how to stir, the delicious world of risottos is right at your fingertips.

Makes 4 servings

1 bunch asparagus, about 1 pound
1 tablespoon butter
½ cup finely chopped yellow onion
1 cup uncooked Arborio rice
½ cup dry white wine
6 cups low-sodium chicken broth, warmed
1 cup freshly grated Parmigiano-Reggiano cheese, plus more for serving
zest of 1 lemon
salt and black pepper
4 pint-size Mason jars

Bring a pot of lightly salted water to a boil. Trim the bottom inch or so off the asparagus stalks and add the stalks to the boiling water. Cook briefly until they turn bright green, 1 or 2 minutes. Transfer the asparagus to in an ice-water bath for about a minute. Remove and cut into 1-inch pieces.

In a medium saucepan over medium heat, melt the butter. Add the onion and cook until translucent. Add the rice and stir until it begins to turn translucent but remains white in the center. Pour in the white wine and cook until it has mostly evaporated.

Using a ladle, add ½ cup broth to the rice. Stir until the rice has absorbed most of the liquid, then add an additional ½ cup broth and continue stirring. Repeat. After 3 cups of broth have been added, stir in the asparagus and then return to adding broth. When the rice is al dente, after 20 to 25 minutes, stir in the grated cheese and lemon zest; season to taste with salt and pepper. Let cool and then spoon the risotto into Mason jars with more grated Parmigiano-Reggiano and a grinding of black pepper on top. Seal and refrigerate until ready to use.

squash risotto

Butternut squash is fantastic in the fall, but it has a delicate taste and needs the right recipes to stand out. Here, the nutty, sweet taste and soft texture of the squash is highlighted by the simplicity of the risotto.

Makes 4 servings

6 cups low-sodium chicken broth, warmed

1 tablespoon olive oil

1 package fresh butternut squash, about 1 pound, cut into 1-inch cubes

1 tablespoon butter

¼ cup finely chopped yellow onion

1 cup uncooked Arborio rice

½ cup dry white wine

1 cup freshly grated Parmigiano-Reggiano cheese, divided

salt and black pepper

fresh sage leaves, for garnish

4 pint-size Mason jars

Heat the chicken broth in a saucepan over medium heat.

Heat the olive oil in a skillet over medium heat. Add the squash and cook for 5 to 10 minutes, until it softens and turns golden. Transfer to a plate and set aside.

Melt the butter in a medium saucepan or pot over medium heat. Add the onion and cook until translucent. Add the rice and stir until it starts to turn translucent but remains white in the center. Pour in the white wine and cook until it has mostly evaporated.

Now it's time to start adding the broth. Using a ladle, add ½ cup broth to the rice. Stir until the rice has absorbed most of the liquid, then add another ½ cup broth. Continue adding broth in this fashion, making sure to keep stirring. As it absorbs the liquid, the rice will start to soften.

After you've added about 3 cups of broth, stir in the squash. Continue adding broth, ½ cup at a time, until the risotto has reached the al dente stage, about 20 minutes. Reserve any leftover broth for another use.

As a last step, stir in ¾ cup grated cheese and salt and pepper to taste. The risotto should have a creamy consistency, not too sticky. Once it's seasoned to your liking, serve it for dinner garnished with more Parmigiano and some sage leaves. Or, let it cool and then spoon it into Mason jars with more Parmigiano sprinkled on top. Garnish with sage leaves, seal, and refrigerate. Reheat in a bowl or on a plate.

porcini mushroom risotto

When it gets cold and fresh vegetables are scarce, mushrooms come to the rescue. Porcinis have a warm, earthy flavor that I find irresistible and they work perfectly in a creamy risotto.

Makes 4 servings

¾ ounce dried porcini mushrooms

1 cup hot water

1 tablespoon butter

½ cup finely chopped yellow onion

1 cup uncooked Arborio rice

½ cup dry white wine

5 cups low-sodium chicken broth, warmed

1 cup freshly grated Parmigiano-Reggiano cheese, plus more for serving

salt and black pepper

4 pint-size Mason jars

In a small bowl, combine the mushrooms with the hot water. Let sit for 30 minutes. Remove the rehydrated mushrooms from the water, reserving the liquid to use in the risotto. Chop the mushrooms and set aside.

In a medium saucepan, melt the butter over medium heat. Add the chopped onion and cook until it becomes translucent. Add the rice and stir until it begins to turn translucent but remains white in the center. Pour in the white wine and cook until it has mostly evaporated.

Using a ladle, add ½ cup broth to the rice. Stir until the rice has absorbed most of the liquid, then repeat. After you've added about 2 cups of broth, ½ cup at a time, add the mushrooms and continue to stir. When it's time to add more liquid, this time ladle in ½ cup of the mushroom-soaking water instead of broth, making sure to avoid any mushroom grit from the bottom of the bowl.

Keep stirring and adding broth until the rice is al dente and the risotto is creamy, usually after about 5 cups of broth. Stir in 1 cup grated cheese and season to taste with salt and pepper; remove from the heat and let cool. Spoon into jars, top with some more Parmigiano, seal, and refrigerate until ready to use. Reheat in a bowl or on a plate before eating.

snacks and dips

Mason jars are perfect for transporting snacks. Fill them with these dips and spreads to help you get through your workday, turn a long car ride into a pleasant excursion, and make you a hit at the next party or picnic you attend.

bruschetta

It never ceases to amaze me how bruschetta, with so few ingredients, can taste so delicious. Bruschetta is a celebration of the tomato, a delicious and healthy snack on a slice of bread.

Makes 4 servings

5 vine-ripened tomatoes, diced
1 garlic clove, finely chopped
7 or 8 large basil leaves, julienne-cut into strips
2 tablespoons olive oil
salt and black pepper
ciabatta or French baguette slices, lightly toasted
4 half-pint Mason jars

In a medium bowl, mix together the tomatoes, garlic, basil, olive oil, and salt and pepper to taste. Cover and refrigerate for 30 minutes to let the flavors come together. Place the mixture in a Mason jar, seal, and refrigerate. Bring it to work along with some bread slices in a zip-top plastic bag. Add healthy spoonfuls of bruschetta to the bread and enjoy.

mango salsa

Mango salsa quickly became a favorite of mine because of the mix of sweet flavors with crunchy bell pepper and onion. If you've never tried a mango salsa before, you're in for a treat!

Makes 4 servings

2 mangoes (or 3 if small), finely cubed*
½ red bell pepper, finely diced
¼ red onion, finely diced
2 tablespoons chopped fresh cilantro
2 jalapeño chiles, finely diced
juice of ½ lime
salt and black pepper
tortilla chips, for dipping
4 half-pint Mason jars

* For mango-cubing directions, see the recipe for Curry Chicken Salad on page 85.

In a medium bowl, mix together the mangoes, bell pepper, onion, cilantro, and jalapeños. Stir in the lime juice, season to taste with salt and pepper, and stir again. Cover and refrigerate for 30 minutes to let the flavors come together before serving. Serve, or transfer to Mason jars, seal, and refrigerate. Bring tortilla chips to work in a bag or another jar to eat with the salsa.

guacamole

I personally believe that guacamole is pretty much the best thing on the planet. I love this take on the classic version. The grapefruit adds a great citrus kick, and its mild bitterness perfectly complements the spiciness of the chiles and the creaminess of the avocado.

Makes 4 servings

½ grapefruit

3 avocados

½ red onion, finely chopped

2 jalapeño chiles, finely chopped

¼ cup chopped fresh cilantro

juice of ½ lime

salt and black pepper

tortilla chips, for dipping

4 half-pint mason jars

Section the half grapefruit and slice into 1-inch pieces. Cut the avocados in half, discard the pits, and scoop out the flesh. Place in a large bowl and mash with a wooden spoon to the desired consistency, leaving the avocados a little chunky. Mix in the grapefruit pieces, onion, jalapeños, cilantro, and lime juice along with a generous pinch of salt and pepper. Taste and add more salt and pepper as needed. Transfer the guacamole to a Mason jar, seal, and refrigerate until you're ready to eat it. Bring tortilla chips in another jar or a bag for dipping.

spicy salsa

This salsa is great when you really want a kick. You can up the ante by using different types of peppers—I recommend a habanero if you're feeling dangerous.

Makes 4 servings

5 plum tomatoes
10 green onions (white part only)
2 jalapeño chiles, halved and seeded
½ cup chopped fresh cilantro
juice from 2 or 3 limes
2 tablespoons bottled hot pepper sauce
1 teaspoon garlic powder
1 teaspoon black pepper
salt
tortilla chips, for dipping
4 half-pint mason jars

In the bowl of a food processor, combine the tomatoes, green onions, jalapeños, cilantro, lime juice, hot pepper sauce, garlic powder, and black pepper. Process until everything is finely chopped. Taste and add salt, if needed. Using a funnel, pour the salsa into a Mason jar, then seal and refrigerate. Serve with chips (bring them to work in a jar or bag).

spicy hummus and vegetables

There's no better midday snack than veggies with hummus—and the great thing about this snack is that you don't need separate containers for the dip and the vegetables. All you have to do is plant your veggies upright in the dip, close the Mason jar, and *voilà*, you have something to see you through the afternoon at work.

Makes 4 servings

1 (15-ounce) can chickpeas, rinsed and drained

5 to 6 tablespoons olive oil, as needed

1 clove garlic, roughly chopped

3 tablespoons tahini

½ teaspoon salt

½ teaspoon black pepper

6 tablespoons lemon juice

1 teaspoon red pepper flakes

celery and carrots, for dipping

4 half-pint Mason jars

Place the chickpeas in the bowl of a food processor along with 5 tablespoons of the olive oil. Add the garlic, tahini, salt, pepper, lemon juice, and red pepper flakes. Process to blend the ingredients together. If needed to achieve the desired smooth consistency, add another tablespoon of olive oil.

Cut the celery and carrots into strips that will fit into the Mason jar with the top closed. Scoop ½ cup of hummus into the bottom of the jar and then set the vegetable strips upright in the hummus. Seal the jar and refrigerate until ready to use.

red pepper and feta dip

Roasting red peppers is fun, because you get to turn a tough, crunchy vegetable into something soft and sweet. It's like magic! Puréeing the roasted peppers together with feta and spicy red pepper flakes makes a great dip that's both sweet and tangy.

This dip is easy to make; the most intensive part of the process is roasting the peppers. If you don't have time to do that, you can buy roasted peppers instead; a 16-ounce jar should do the trick.

Makes 4 servings

4 red bell peppers
2 garlic cloves
1½ cups, about 9 ounces, crumbled feta cheese
¼ cup olive oil
1 teaspoon red pepper flakes
¼ teaspoon cayenne pepper
2 tablespoons lemon juice
salt and black pepper
pita bread or chips, for dipping
4 half-pint Mason jars

Under a broiler or on a grill, roast the whole red peppers, rotating the peppers, until the skins have blistered and blackened on all sides. This should take about 5 minutes per side. Remove and place in a brown paper bag; close the bag and let sit for 15 minutes while the peppers cool. Then pull off the pepper skins, cut off the stems, and remove the seeds. Slice the peppers into strips and place in the bowl of a food processor.

Roughly slice the garlic and add to the food processor with the roasted peppers. Add the feta cheese, olive oil, red pepper flakes, cayenne pepper, lemon juice, and black pepper to taste. Process until smooth, taste, and adjust the seasoning with salt and pepper as desired. Spoon the dip into Mason jars, seal, and refrigerate until ready to use. Bring along pita bread or chips to accompany the dip.

salad dressings

I love to use vinaigrettes for my Mason jar salads because they're simple to make yet delicious. Other dressings often require many more ingredients, and they can separate in the jar. If you're not using store-bought dressings, then vinaigrettes are the way to go.

There are just three basic parts to a vinaigrette—acid, oil, and seasoning—but the key to success is ensuring that all the ingredients emulsify. Start by putting your vinegar or citrus juice (the acid) in a bowl with your seasonings (salt, pepper, and whatever else you're including). Whisk and then slowly add the olive oil, bit by bit. Continue whisking as you add oil until the dressing comes together and thickens. (If you prefer, you can also mix your dressing in a blender.)

Another secret to making a great vinaigrette is to buy high-quality olive oil. Once you start using really good olive oil, you'll never want to go back.

These recipes should make enough dressing for one or two salads, depending on how much dressing you like to use.

french vinaigrette

2 tablespoons lemon juice
½ tablespoon minced shallot
¼ teaspoon Dijon mustard
pinch of salt
freshly ground black pepper, to taste
3 tablespoons olive oil

Whisk together the lemon juice, shallot, mustard, salt, and pepper. Slowly add the olive oil, whisking, until the dressing thickens.

red wine vinaigrette

2 tablespoons red wine vinegar
½ tablespoon minced shallot
pinch of salt
freshly ground black pepper, to taste
3 tablespoons olive oil

Whisk together the vinegar, shallot, salt, and pepper. Slowly add the olive oil, whisking, until the dressing thickens.

lemon vinaigrette

2 tablespoons lemon juice
pinch of salt
freshly ground black pepper, to taste
3 tablespoons olive oil

Whisk together the lemon juice, salt, and pepper. Slowly add the olive oil, whisking, until the dressing thickens.

lime vinaigrette

2 tablespoons lime juice
1 tablespoon chopped fresh cilantro
pinch of salt
freshly ground black pepper, to taste
dash of hot sauce (optional)
3 tablespoons olive oil

Whisk together the lime juice, cilantro, salt, pepper, and hot sauce (if using). Slowly add the olive oil, whisking, until the dressing thickens.

sherry vinaigrette

2½ tablespoons sherry vinegar
pinch of salt
freshly ground black pepper, to taste
3 tablespoons olive oil

Whisk together the vinegar, salt, and pepper. Slowly add the olive oil, whisking, until the dressing thickens.

balsamic vinaigrette

1 tablespoon balsamic vinegar
1 teaspoon honey
pinch of salt
freshly ground black pepper, to taste
3 tablespoons olive oil

Whisk together the vinegar, honey, salt, and pepper. Slowly add the olive oil, whisking, until the dressing thickens.

blueberry vinaigrette

3 tablespoons fresh blueberries
2 tablespoons apple cider vinegar
¼ teaspoon honey
pinch of salt
freshly ground black pepper, to taste
4 to 5 tablespoons olive oil

Place the blueberries, vinegar, honey, salt, and pepper in a blender and blend until smooth. With the blender running, slowly add the olive oil until it is the right consistency.

apple cider vinaigrette with honey

2 tablespoons apple cider vinegar
½ teaspoon honey
pinch of salt
freshly ground black pepper, to taste
3 tablespoons olive oil

Whisk together the vinegar, honey, salt, and pepper. Slowly add the olive oil, whisking, until the dressing thickens.

white wine vinaigrette

2 tablespoons white wine vinegar
pinch of salt
freshly ground black pepper, to taste
3 tablespoons olive oil
Whisk together the vinegar, salt, and pepper. Slowly add the olive oil, whisking, until the dressing thickens.

citrus-soy vinaigrette

2 tablespoons orange juice

1 tablespoon unseasoned rice wine vinegar

¼ teaspoon soy sauce

1 teaspoon honey

freshly ground black pepper, to taste

4 tablespoons olive oil

Whisk together the orange juice, vinegar, soy sauce, honey, and pepper. Slowly add the olive oil, whisking, until the dressing thickens.

Common Conversions

1 gallon = 4 quarts = 8 pints = 16 cups = 128 fluid ounces = 3.8 liters

1 quart = 2 pints = 4 cups = 32 ounces = .95 liter

1 pint = 2 cups = 16 ounces = 480 ml

1 cup = 8 ounces = 240 ml

¼ cup = 4 tablespoons = 12 teaspoons = 2 ounces = 60 ml

1 tablespoon = 3 teaspoons = ½ fluid ounce = 15 ml

Temperature Conversions

Fahrenheit (°F)	Celsius (°C)
200°F	95°C
225°F	110°C
250°F	120°C
275°F	135°C
300°F	150°C
325°F	165°C
350°F	175°C
375°F	190°C
400°F	200°C
425°F	220°C
450°F	230°C
475°F	245°C

Volume Conversions

U.S.	U.S. equivalent	Metric
1 tablespoon (3 teaspoons)	½ fluid ounce	15 milliliters
¼ cup	2 fluid ounces	60 milliliters
⅓ cup	3 fluid ounces	90 milliliters
½ cup	4 fluid ounces	120 milliliters
⅔ cup	5 fluid ounces	150 milliliters
¾ cup	6 fluid ounces	180 milliliters
1 cup	8 fluid ounces	240 milliliters
2 cups	16 fluid ounces	480 milliliters

Weight Conversions

U.S.	Metric
½ ounce	15 grams
1 ounce	30 grams
2 ounces	60 grams
¼ pound	115 grams
⅓ pound	150 grams
½ pound	225 grams
¾ pound	350 grams
1 pound	450 grams

index

acknowledgments

Thank you to Kyle, for believing in me, brainstorming with me, taste testing for me, and for editing everything I wrote. You support me in everything I do and I am better for it.

This book wouldn't be what it is without my parents, who gave me their time, their kitchen, and all of their weekends during the summer and fall to help me cook food for this book. To my mother, you were tirelessly upbeat when I felt overwhelmed or when there was bad lighting and it seemed the photos would be ruined. Thank you for putting up with all of my planning and thank you for being there for me always.

Thank you to Jess, you were a great sounding board and taste tester. Plus, these photos wouldn't be here without you — thank you for letting me borrow your camera!

A huge thank you to all of my friends and family. I couldn't have done it without all the food conversations and support over the last few months. In particular, thank you to Chelsea, for the bulgur wheat idea, to Laura for the gazpacho, and to Kathie for the blueberry salad. Thank you to Kate for the cover photo help, and to Lindsay, who let me talk recipes by the pool. Thank you to Pete for the photography tips and encouragement. Thank you to Zia Ida and the whole Izzo-Veneziano family, who fed me incredible pasta throughout my time in law school, and who taught me that the simple meals are the best meals.

Thank you to the Dupont FRESHFARM Market in Dupont Circle, Washington, DC, and to the Bardstown Road farmers' market in Louisville, Kentucky — I used your produce in all of my meals and took the advice of many of your farmers.

Finally, thank you to Kelly Reed, my editor, who saw my blog and thought I was good enough to become an author, to Kourtney Joy for publicizing my book, and to the Ulysses Press team (especially Phyllis Elving) who edited my manuscript and photos — I would not have written a cookbook without you. Thank you for giving me this incredible opportunity.

about the author

Julia Mirabella grew up in a household that emphasized Italian food and taught her to love cooking with fresh ingredients. When starting her first job as an attorney, she realized she needed to rethink her work lunches and started making Mason jar salads as a way of eating better. You can follow her blog at www.myfoodandotherstuff.com. She lives in Washington, D.C.